WALKING THROUGH THE JUNGLE

WALKING THROUGH THE JUNGLE

Illustrated by Debbie Harter

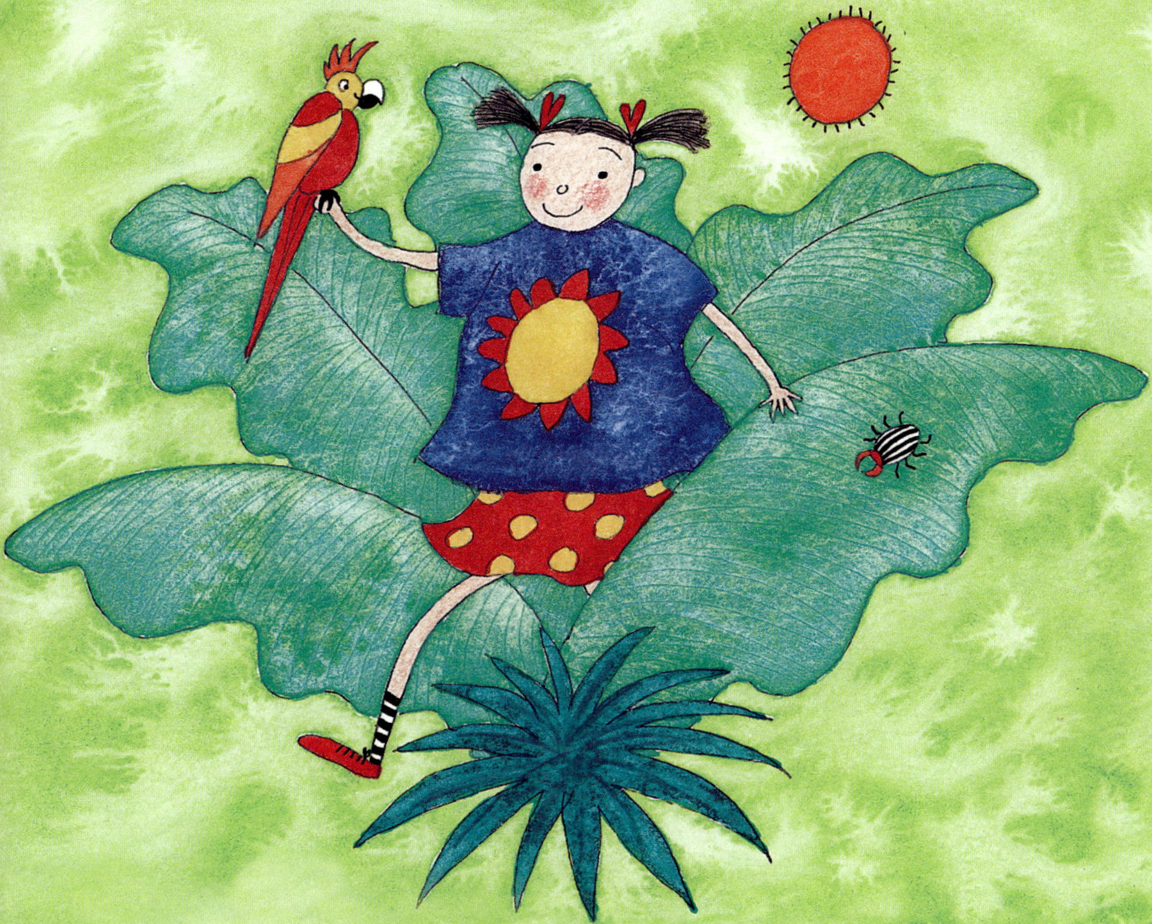

Heinemann

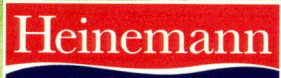

Walking through the jungle,
Walking through the jungle,

What do you see?
What do you see?

Chasing after me,
Chasing after me.

Floating on the ocean,
Floating on the ocean,

What do you see?
What do you see?

I think I see a whale,

Chasing after me,
Chasing after me.

Climbing in the mountains,
Climbing in the mountains,

What do you see?
What do you see?

Chasing after me,
Chasing after me.

I think I see a crocodile,

Snap! Snap! Snap!

Chasing after me,
Chasing after me.

Trekking in the desert,
Trekking in the desert,

What do you see?
What do you see?

Chasing after me,
Chasing after me.

Slipping on the iceberg,
Slipping on the iceberg,

What do you see?
What do you see?

I think I see a polar bear,

Growl
Growl
Growl!

Chasing after me,
Chasing after me.

Running home for supper,
Running home for supper,

Where have you been?
Where have you been?

I've been around the world and back,
I've been around the world and back,

And guess what I've seen,
And guess what I've seen.